WISHBONE

DON SHARE

WISHBONE

*For Leslie, so
this you so
much for reading
poets?*

A BLACK SPARROW BOOK

DAVID R. GODINE · *Publisher* · *Boston*

This is
A Black Sparrow Book
published in 2012 by
David R. Godine, Publisher
Post Office Box 450
Jaffrey, New Hampshire 03452
www.blacksparrowbooks.com

The Black Sparrow Books pressmark is by Julian Waters
www.waterslettering.com

LIBRARY OF CONGRESS CATALOGING-IN-PUBLICATION DATA

Share, Don, 1957–
Wishbone / Don Share.
p. cm.
ISBN 978-1-57423-219-6
I. Title.
PS3569.H3423W57 2012
811'.54—dc22
2011017584

First Edition
Printed in the United States

This work remembers Leonard and Lulu.

*With love to John Hennessy, Aram Saroyan, David Shapiro,
and above all, Jacquelyn Pope.*

CONTENTS

III.

IV.

I

THE CREW CHANGE

Hobo, Bono, bone heap.
I mutilate dandelions in the sun,
rattle my rake like a saber

when Michelle-my-neighbor,
over compost, opines
that *Aqualung*'s a classic;

"At least I think so. U2?"
Does she mean: me, too?
In the foul rag and compost pile

of my creaky abdomen I rustle
all the leaves of my locomotive breath
to agree because anything you say,

Michelle, must be so! We live
in a time of need. Your hair always
looks brushed. Our conversations

are abrupt. And yet . . .
The children grow and play over time
like centipedes behind our sofas;

the tools I never use seem
delightful on their pegs in the shed,
like the hopes I sharpened

once beside the gleaming rails
as a schoolboy, a hiker, a little hobo never
far from someone's backyard trampoline.

On Smoking out Some Bees with a Flaming Torch

The eye of the nest, black and invisible.
It's like that for safekeeping.

The smoke is played
by the wind on its lyre.

The bees moan at that new dust,
and my gloves and bucket

hum the same sort
of *damn-you* gibberish.

If I had a nest myself like this,
I would go to it

even in this cloud,
because nothing escapes

the hand that reaches for it.

To An Eye Infection

Blood-orange red at dusk,
an ache in the orbit of the eye.

Lassitude in a way
·not to see

well at all:
no reading, no judging.

I need a scientist
of the body –

I have my
wallet ready.

Ask the history detective:
Why hunger

for food, for peace,
when I can't see the writing

on the wall?
Irascible inflammation!

The ophthalmologist's
dissecting blue needlepuffs.

And at last, a tiny phial
which I uncap to release

tiny prescription tears.

Rice in the Spoon

Each in his house,
thinking of the key,

the locks, the windows,
doors, and roof.

In my sleep I lift
a finger. I see . . .

opposing blocks,
like Legos, in painful

composure of modes,
not moods.

Fake red feathers
fluffed in a spotted vase.

Sea glass beached
on a porch bench.

A brown bust
of a sad man.

A huge tin pitcher,
parched for years.

Rice glued to
a badly washed spoon.

Even the dust
quit moving to settle.

Even the snow is
a qualm, a sea.

In Intensive Care

There's a white
elephant in every
living room.

He eludes you,
as all confessionalists
elude you.

He wears an I MAKE
MY OWN STINK
BAIT T-shirt.

He's alone
with his thoughts,
but where are they?

He's rich
because his pockets
are full of the past.

He kites
checks to both Yeats
and Keats.

When he flies,
he leaves his wallet
on the seat.

When he dies,
he lies down in
a hole, to forget.

There but
for the grace
of Dad, go I.

ON SCREAMING YOUR HEAD OFF

The voices of my world were not tender and unquestioning.
                                                    W. S. Di Piero

Drink your ass off, scream your head off! It's why
God gave you that molecule of his indecipherable wrath.

When you calm down again, talk to me. Sorry,
I have to go where my skin goes, an empath

out of sympathy with himself who has to overcome
this shitty cold to go Easter egg hunting, lordy me.

The letter I would write to my daughter is not
the letter I would write to my wife. "Dear Wife,"

I'd say, "When you calm down again, talk to me."
I've stopped getting haircuts, I wear muddy shoes

and rumpled clothes, sport a fresh chip on my shoulder.
But the worst thing is . . . not wanting to fly:

of all impossible things, the most impossible.
I turn up hopelessly late – at airports, at parties,

for work, and frankly, I'm better late than never.
When you calm down again, talk to me, OK?

Wild anything, fishy screamer, I'll tell you a tale
of the Yo-Semite I yam, of my pyrrhic experience as a seer.

I'm . . . a slow learner . . . entirely self-taught. I lie.
I'm a glaciologist of gloom, which is as bad as it sounds,

so cue the engrams! Send in the clowns!
We had a love-hate relationship on a sinking ship.

16

But I'm ready to settle in a library of hills, I'm willing
to drink sequoia wine, guzzle sequoia blood

among the squirrels, happy to write my woody gospel.
When you calm down again, remember wordy me.

THE ESCAPE MINISTRY

(with lines from *Southern Living* and Dante's *Purgatory*)

Apricots are in season . . . Now what?
The season is short, maybe eight weeks, tops.
Plant a row for the hungry. I never

understand why people risk a biscuit
to baking powder; I am the self-rising
White Lily, and my wall is covered

with rug beaters! I own no
unrealistic tropical plants.
The piano belonged to my grandmother.

My parents were poor grad students,
but Mom still got me a fancy Steiff
rabbit for Easter, bless her.

I just like pigs, and my recipe
for priest's pancakes has been
in the family for generations.

You have to eat them quickly,
because they deflate.
We think the original owners

kept farm animals here.
May I offer you a chocolate?
The farm chicks all say:

"Live well, laugh often, cook much!"
There's some bacon in the kitchen.
Nothing could be more blissful.

The eyes of the envious
are stitched shut with wire.

On Imaginary and Scarecrow Sins at Home

I never broke loose
from the copyholds

was a man
counting silently

not passing the time
as it was passing me

everything was of the moment
fallen on hard times yet

still possessed
of wit and intelligence

I was an inspector
in the wife trade

and had all the zeal
of a disbeliever

CIVILIZATION AND ITS DISCONTENTS

I've never sent a telegram,
and now it's too late!

PAUL BLACKBURN'S TREE

I have been a fool
    to nature all my life,
as when her knee slid
    so smooth down
the other knee
    and capitulation led
to recapitulation – then:
    "I'll see you back
in the city."
    Clamorous. Mobile.
Jizz is the term
    for a bird's *this-*
ness, its *instress*. That is,
    the way a bird
generally gets out of the way.

But where is the real bird,
    the one in front of us?
Much depends on whatever
    you grew up with –
the birds that flickered
    in front of you, as well
as those you hold close
    to your breast.
I am drawn to you.
    A very simple device,
our crossing paths; our songs
    are heard by no one
but us, and here, and only here,
    just this once.

Ready for a Psalm of My Own

Welcome to the neurogothic! The heart-
break of its crime, the bad breath, the not
knowing how to walk down a sidewalk,
or ways to be polite on public transport-

ation. But it's the sales tax and gang
signs that do us in, the palimpsest ruins
of cardboard box factories, trainyards, stock-
yards, e.g., Bubble Creek, where the blood-

worms still wait for their meal of offal
and bribes. What language do you speak
into your iPhone? What possesses you
to sit there with your mouth half-awful-

open, waiting for another text or lottery
ticket? Go ahead, flip to the sports section,
red-eyed: we're a nation of newspaper
readers, still waiting for the Blago verdict,

waiting on the Green Line train to Harlem
and Lake, waiting for climate change
when it already has. The shekel stops
here! I'm done praying daily for the souls

of the commuting dead, the soon-to-be-
unemployed, for Christ among the olives,
and Dad amid the tombstones. I've my
umbrella out and Cubs cap on, I'm curious-

ly Odyssean in the Loop, the very definition
of hideous. If I were any less resiliant, I
would have to be a murderer: nature here
has abandoned all hope of shaping a man.

FORTUNE

Gunmen come
from homes
with nice
china

HWÆT!

after Rilke

Who among the angels would hear me
if I started screaming my head off?

BOWLING ON THE DAY OF ATONEMENT

My old man used to say
a little rain never hurt anybody.

There were downpours
at his funeral.

ON FIXING THINGS

I tap-smashed – by mistake? –
our bedroom window, and rational-
ized it as a large weep-

hole that winter, for a while, at least,
until the mist from the ends of
the earth gathered there, and till

glass icicles slivered into our toes
and fingers too many times
to ignore any longer –

Do we get the new pane cut
to be slightly larger or smaller,
how to remove the old sharp shards

with their dangerous forget-
fulnesses, and how will we fit
in the glaze and points? This is the kind

of thing your dad knew without thinking,
but he's dead now and can't tell us a thing.
Even worse, it's Sunday, the one day

we have to rest as well as work, so . . .
Time to wrestle with the new glass
at long last, and I wake up early,

start to shave: with a swift, near-
knowing stroke, his old razor deftly
measures a long crisp cut across my neck.

What will stop me now from bleeding
clear, sharp air? How can an inch
of trauma measure eternity, ever?

Who was this saint of glass?

ON THANKSGIVING

The Lord gave us tears to shed. . . . Do not try to stem their flow.
                                                                    Maimonides

It sleeps in the cradle more or less as it sleeps in the grave;
It doesn't mean a heavy hammer, as might be expected,
    but a small workman's tool.*
It's each woman not being built like another;
It's coital small talk as well as full-bore hypochondria;
It's reading the classics and feeling high-handed and heady;
It doesn't love truth and is right not to love it;
It's being boyish and not in control of oneself;
It is a glass of red wine, and a glass of even redder wine;
It's the sudden piercing look of a teacher;
It is a tattoo on a brother's arm that says, *Out of Luck*;
It is eating clumsily, sleeping poorly, and waking at last;
It's buying a magnolia when you really wanted a dogwood;
It's beginning to feel like an old man so long
    after imagining what it would be like;
It is the existence of the soul, long thought abandoned;
It is the onion, of the lily family, that my ancestors
    once pined for in the wilderness.

* *Interpreter's Dictionary of the Bible* (1962), v. K-Q, p. 215, reworded slightly; other
inspiration from *The Goncourt Journals*.

ON BEING PHILOSOPHICAL

My tendency is to be philosophical before
I even need to be philosophical, which is,
perhaps, the essence of *the thing itself.*

Taking a break from work, for example,
to worry about losing my job,
I ponder why one uses the figure

of a dog thrown a crumb from the table –
what dog relishes a crumb? No, boss,
morsel is the better word (bone, gristle,

chunk, shred, hunk): dogs require
things to devour, being devout gulpers
who by nature leave behind essential drool.

You can't fool a dog with your crumbs.
That's the heart of it, the meat of it.
What you toss they'll jaw up well.

This is muscular, nervy, an act
that contains and embodies its own
completion because dogs do

a great job of waiting, unlike Descartes
or me, needing no mind behind the mind.
Like Descartes, I keep deciding

that foreboding is worth something.
So I eat numberless vegetables to avoid
injury to fellow souls, in spite

of which I am not a virtuous man.
Dogs don't converse while they eat.
We say grace, clink glasses, drink the wine.

Where there's a will, evidently there's . . . a *will*.

STONECROP

In the crop of stone,
your ink was ripe.

Like stonecrop
with no stone,

the dying inherit
the dead, cut

what they can't
untie. They chew

but never swallow:
God alone is full.

It saw what is fragile
break.

ANOTHER LONG POEM

The tell-tale
heart
is mine.

CRUXOLA

About suffering she was never wrong,
the old mistress, how we reached a crux
and moved on, a pathos not mentioned
because it is the whole of the story.

My bearded double with the English accent
devoured *Middlemarch* in the middle
of this life, got a cot in the Cottswolds,
some cheese in chalky Cheshire,

An ox in Oxfordshire, met with a don
in London, got unhinged at Stonehenge,
and sought to avoid the errors and sorrows,

The spellings, contradictions, and virgules
of the original. He got purchase on
a pile of rare books, drank the milk
of human kindness, and asked the age-

Old question, is there a right
to remain silent? He even hypermilled
and walked oddly to avoid
crushing ants: he became

Very Zen and wrote himself off.

ON RADICAL HOPE

It may be that great sorrows are not all mute.
And it may be they are.
Pierre Reverdy

Not only bi-polar, but polar,
You ask the farm-family tour-teen whether
Chickens or eggs came first in the taxonomic hay.
What is the poor overalled thing to say?
The things you fuss over.

Ghost, ether, ectoplasm, mirror.
Wax. Film. Sloppy thrownness, love and sleep.
(I think a few of these are actually from Heidegger.)
The soul is self-moving, has the withinness (*Sure!*)
Of withinness, is an un-winglike thing. *Cheep.*

The thread has come off your needle
Again, the dragonfly is snared in the screen,
And the whole world aches again and again.
Who put the ache into Blake? Needless
To ask, to have the last word, because

Like the child who feverishly draws
Happy houses, one after the other,
I don't mind if the culpa is all mea:
The crow of plenty caws,
I can't father anyone the way you mother

Everyone, and anyhow what part
Of mañana don't you understand?
My thumb leaves a sweaty moon
On a color plate in *The History of Art*;
I teach Maddy how to make castles in sand

And find myself feeling flighty.
How the fallen are mighty.

DIE WELT IS SO VERKEHRT

Sorry to be
the one to tell you,
but your emotions
have been hacked.

Epitaph

Stockbrokers who live after us,
Don't harden your hearts to us.
If you pity poor devils like us,
Maybe God will show more mercy to you.
You see the five or six of us hanging here –
As for the guts we stuffed so well,
By now they are devoured and decayed,
And we, our bones, converted to ashes and dust.
Don't you laugh at our expense
But pray to God he absolves us all.

We call you brothers – don't scoff!
So what if Justice sent us to death?
Not everybody has such good sense.
Speak up for us, now that we can't,
Before the Son of the Virgin,
So his mercy to us never runs dry
But saves us each from burning in Hell.
We are dead. Please don't taunt us
But pray to God he absolves us all.

The rain has washed and bathed us.
The sun has dried and blackened us.
Magpies and crows have pecked out our eyes,
Plucked each hair from our brows and beards.
We can't even get a moment of rest –
Back and forth we swing and sway,
Always at the whim of the wind.
Thanks to the birds we're more pitted than thimbles.
So don't join our cozy fraternity
But pray to God he absolves us all.

Prince Jesus, master over all,
Don't let us drop down to Hell.
We have no business in a place like that.
Brokers, believe it – this is no joke –
Pray to God he absolves us all.

POETRY

Rustling
in my own
silks.

THE GOSPEL TRUTH

St. Matthew did not know that mites live
        in our eyelashes,
or he'd not have indicted us for our
        motes and beams.
Every character in my name a mark
        of resolves, notwithstanding
all I have is a forlorn inclination –
        but even that seems to be bent.
The strips of insulation in the attic hang
        down, flayed and torn.
We need a new border, and ought to poison
        the chickweed before it goes dormant.
Where is he, meanwhile, who will save us,
        wound in his side?
The one who knows is off on another
        job, collecting taxes, impervious
to the indignity of having been reborn.

THE TRAUMATOPHILE

> *We all take the anger*
> *We all take disappointment*
> *We all take everything*
> Six-year old girl singing in her bath

If the dogs would stop barking
If the kids would quit squawking
If the cats would stop pooping
Then I'd study war no more

If the via were no longer dolorosa
If God still cared for tithes of potherds
If the Magnificent Mile were still mag
Then I'd study war no more

If Adam were still the first of men
If the underthought were not the self-holocaust
If busy curios would thirsting fly
Then I'd study war no more

If we could unsphere the spirit of Plato
If you could ignore the knock on the door in a dream
If white noise kept away the person from Porlock
Then I'd study war no more

If your purple butterfly were still a heartfriend
If my mirror were too young to know God
If gentleness were the same as kindness
Then I'd study war no more

If my first wife would call once a decade
If I were not the patron saint of neurotic women
If the straggling bees would quit dying on my porch
Then I'd study war no more

If I could get these stitches out sooner
If hurricanes ran out of the alphabet
If the furnace guy could get the heat going
Then I'd study war no more

If the thief would close the gate behind him
If the pilot light would stay on
If our basement spiders could spare the centipedes
Then I'd study war no more

If all the syllables in the world could put us back together
    again
If I had a "life's work" (what did I expect?)
If moms weren't so maxed-out
Then I'd study war no more

If I could take salt from the press of the sea
If I had that old cedar chest back with whatever was in it
If the natural consequence of moving for love were not
    bad credit
Then I'd study war no more

If I could remember that quiet amniotic swish
If my stitches did not have so many itches
If they would not quiver in my skin like tuning forks
Then I'd study war no more

WISHBONE

I have a bone to pick
with whoever runs this joint.
I don't much like
being stuck out in the rain
just to feed on the occasional
vole or baby rabbit
and these wet weed-salads
confound my intestines.
A cat can't throw himself
into the Des Plaines River,
not even in the luscious fall.
I get yelled at in human
language every single day
for things I can't begin
to comprehend, let alone change.
But I go on cleaning myself –
why shouldn't I? –
and so I think I smell sweet,
even though I suspect otherwise.
I wouldn't harm a fly normally,
but why doesn't anybody
take care of me? How am I
supposed to know that it's Easter,
that I'm not allowed to die
in my own bed, and that neither prong
of this wishbone is meant for me?

MAGNA CARTA

I must be
the Sisyphus,
the king
of rain.

My umbrella
isn't worth
the paper
it's written on.

THE MAN WHO WALKS LIKE ME

Now that my father isn't
around anymore, I'm the guy
at home who has to look old.

I saw a guy just like him
limping around;
I limp around, too.

Shaking out the sheets
of her newspaper
on the plane: an elderly

woman who annoyed the hell
out of me in the adjacent
booth of my lone dumb

sorrow; she harrumphed
like a nightingale who sings, then
sends you the bill.

Meanwhile, it's still light
out, it's still day. I denounce
my own day.

Then I walk out just
like the man who walks
like me. I studied him hard, but

the body is no scientist.

THE GHOST

How did he do it?

He told you precisely

How he does it.

But is this exactly

What he does?

Nobody

Will ever know,

And no one

Can ever say

For certain

Because the truth is –

That's another story.

CASH FOR CLUNKERS

My clunky cat is weary of this life at last.
I see our whole household as endangered
now in the autozone of love and rust.

She didn't even stir when you made
a fish stew, so it must be time
to start praying for her fairytale soul.

I still believe in the electricity of storms,
though rather than ruffle her aging fur they
lighten her all at once, and rebound away –

You'd be surprised, but this is so.

MY OWN BACK YARD

In my own backyard,
I have the idea
that the good will drive
out the bad –
but it never happens.

I was that unfeathered
two-legged thing,
your son:
one of your shapeless
corporeal triplets,

the cause of heritable
daddyweight
and deafness,
the charismatic megafauna
of your love for Ma.

As members of
a walkaway species,
my brother and I began
what (who knew?)
had already begun –

Kids really do see dead people.

ECLIPSE

Her comma-like
eye-
brows.

Simple legs in milk-
white flame,
plush.

Directly
the night
sky,

shy
of its planets,
furrows

its distant
lemons,
and tilts.

One
of your ancestors
must have read

a forbidden book.

THE DOWNLOOK

Nobody knew it was coming, despite the bellwethers
Of data not persisting, weather alerts, laptop seizures
At customs, gravestones sinking as the Des Plaines rises,
The Mars-lander finding a salty environment, cops
Shooting down a lady wielding a crutch, cover-ups
Of air-traffic errors, the Supreme Court of the U.S.
Overturning local gun bans, General Motors shares
Hitting an X-year low, hundreds of new Internet domains,
Paying more and more but getting less and less,
Crib recalls and salmonella-infected jalapeños,
Fat men who have bad sperm (to no one's surprise),
And meddling relatives who produce toxic nuptials.

I didn't maximize my business potential,
I forgot the words to O Say Can You See,
I let Yiddishkeit die, I didn't check my credit score,
I let my frequent flier miles expire,
I let a case of the *seems* plague my aloofened mind.

No unhurried indulgence in objects of fascination,
No flux or reflux of backslash and solidus, can save me.
Achilles didn't amputate his leg to get rid of that vulnerable heel,
Which looms especially large in the suburbs:
These are my objects. These are my subjects.
Inherited furniture heavy as time-stained tombstones.
Laughing, like Greeks and Romans, at paintings.
Pages of journal-entries that are encomia to solitude.

The pleasure of exaggerating painful things.
Being a thorn-in-flesh L-word, losing one place without
        finding another.
Carnivalesque transgressions, high and low.
Why would you want to kill my spirit so?
I who dot my own infinitesimal i, and who
Picked up that old gent's fallen umbrella on the train

And abjured screeching abjectly when the skinny
Businesswoman in the lime-green suit with matching shoes
(Cute but no doubt uncomfortable) trod on my foot
Not once, but twice, without a word of apology?
As a resume for salvation it's not much, but surely a start?

I won't run through the litany, but still . . .
Here comes the wheelchair newspaper man,
Here comes the automated spam about pattycake
In fishnets and "updating my peni$,"
Here comes the epidemic of asthma, of lice,
Go away toxic peanut! No wonder punks
And ancient Egyptians alike shaved their eyebrows!
Empathy comes naturally to children,
Goes away just as naturally in adults,
And so you're off the hook . . .

But I have call waiting and the calls won't wait.
My bookshelves are marmoreal instead of more real.
Like Coleridge (honest!) I've actually dined on red
Herring, and spent a dreadful night in consequence:
Cross-bones of the fish curved into the creepy
Apparition of a scorpion! Thank you for the empty
Bed, the empty box, the empty glass, the empty voicemail:
You don't understand, I know all this by rote

Not by heart, I'm an in-group
Deviant, I'm the guest who looks away
When the bill arrives, I'm the greatest American
Dog, I think I can dance, you're fired,
I want to be a millionaire
And I'm a symbolum of the downlook.

BRIEFS

Sitting Buddha
or shitting Buddha?

The Emperor Claudius
dreams incessantly of fireflies.

The tree of heaven that grows
in Brooklyn is the Ailanthus.

I hope to be dead and gone,
but not in that order.

The Shirt

The shirt, the red checked shirt you gave me
   from the Miasma Supply Co. –
how to thank you for the shirt?
   It's thermal, like the engines
of volcanoes, of our tempers. It makes me
   want to take the shirt
less traveled. It helps cover over
   my hypochondrium,
right below the ribcage, and is proximate
   to my heart, where feelings
of unease pool and overflow. The shirt.

BALLAD OF THE FOOLISH MAN

I wonder if Emily Dickinson knew
about Chicken Little?
Because I forgot to run
the dishwasher last night.
I still can't sort the laundry properly.

If I had a ghost, I'd have given
it up by now, white
as a sheet of paper, rumpled
as a bed. No,
I don't want to tell

tales out of school, but
we were a summer romance once.
Now I'm swinging like
an old garden gate
on its lamentable hinges. My

body is purifying itself
of everything, even itself: the baby
out with its putative bathwater.
Well, a creature never
knows enough about itself.

Back go the nail-and-duct-
tape onto the tip of the caulk tube.
The chips: let them fall where they may.
Or will. Because basically, you know,
I'm withering. Pre-ill.

SYMBIOSIS

The maimed coyote in the wetland
beyond our sunken fence
croaks all night alone.

Is he heartbroken? Why is
it that I think we are alike?
Nothing can appear without

the sting of night, the song, the wound.

HIGH HOLIDAYS

Rabbit fur and hair strewn through the lawns
    of the Midwest!
The famous feral parakeets of Chicago
    are chattering
With cold. I want to drown myself
    out with the roar
Of the greenish river that slices the city
    clean into two.
Nothing pertains, if that's the right word,
    to what I'm hearing:
Little kids singing Benjamin Britten's
    Ceremony of Carols or, if only
In my mind's ear, what I'm able to recall
    of the *Kol Nidre*:
Rushing over the notes, as if in an unearthly
    hurry to get someplace.

IV

.

To the Sister I Never Had

Sleep quiet and smiling and do not hanker
For a perfection that can never come
Louis MacNeice

Sister that I never had, take the initiative, like Eve,
    against nature!
If kindness is its own reward then you have been paid,
    but not repaid
For your love, and because you were never born you are losing
    your mind

And I don't know what the best escape for you is other
    than the gates
Smitten with destruction that lead away from our garden where,
    when
We played as children, you cradled the mallow – *Gossypium*,
    cotton –

In an uprooted case of the slows: I can't help but think back,
    think
Back on your telling me that dry light is the best, the very best,
And your saying, *When I'm gone, say I was fascinated*
    the whole time!

You asked me about the mean streak in the *goyim*, about the faith
Of our faithless fathers, about the untranslatable doom
    of the Yiddish-
Speakers infausting us with their right-to-left letters and flames –

Sister, I respect the ambient and believe in the dove that lifts
    your eyes,
And I am old enough now to apologize to you for the lies I told
To survive you, and I remember you better than people who really

Lived, or those crows on the wire who taught us Hebrew,
    got drunk
As a drum on a pennyworth of settlebrain, and who pulled you
Out of the rolling waters so you could sit in the kitchen highchair

Kicking the legs like a little girl . . . and when you were older,
    which
You never were, you understood all the things I never said
And taught me a little about how to cook for myself; you made

Sure that there were always fresh flowers on the table
    no matter what,
And above all said grace before each meal in a strange language.
You showed me how to dress for success, gave me courage

When my haircuts and skin and nose and belly let me, inevitably,
Down, and you required that I be and remain a *mensch,*
    in exchange
For which you baked the black-and-white cookies I so adored.

But when the earth froze, making burial difficult, you saw to it
That Kaddish was still said by sons for their fathers, and so
The ritual washing continued, and so on, even though the war

Kept up in which those same sons did things that women could
Neither forgive nor understand, and so they repented giving us
Birth, in spite of which all the prayers got said, and on this same

Subject of the departed I thought it only a small sin to have held
You beautiful even when, especially when, you were angry. God
Why did you make off with the only sister I never had when

There was so much more I could have learned from her, including
How to stay human no matter what? Sister, you hugged me
    when you
Were mad even when the crust didn't come out right
    and your joints

Really ached, and your heart, too, and it's as if I interrupted
A dreamer saying all this now, and in such relative freedom:
Sooner or later even salamanders stop burning, so my dear,

I throw myself on your mercy now that I can't get you
To speak! Once, the boy I was tried to explore some of your heart
Which was perched out on the black bowed tension wires
    running

Through our backyard, and you said *Here*, and I then
    and only then
Could comprehend your Bible and cookbook, left open forever
On the table – you were, well, so brutally practical, saying

Sometimes *Many hands make light work* and sometimes
    on the other
Hand, *Too many cooks spoil the soup*, and nothing made you
    more crazy
Than my being sick, which happened a lot, for which I am sorry.

There was a newspaper headline I saw on the train one day,
I couldn't see the whole thing but it started out: *Science
Uncovers Clue to Mystery of . . .* What was the mystery?

I never found out, which you thought was very funny.
But now that I try to remember you I realize how sad it was that
You spent almost every night teaching yourself how to knit

Impossible dilemmas together . . . You made yourself into a great
Cook of seething stews and heavy loaves, and above all you loved
To call the kettle black. And when you were tearfully hanging

The X-mas lights that last year we spent together you said
Honey, most Jews have had a longer journey than Odysseus
So put down that book, will you? Which made me laugh

Because our father was born in Detroit, and when you were a girl
You pronounced it Troy: where all the men fell, and somehow you
Tunneled from your nightmares all the way to theirs
    as well as mine

In successive choirs because you were never born but I was.

Flip Flops and Mary Janes

If there's a bend, I'm going round it.
Nobody wants to die on a train,
but you're reading *Best
New Horror* when I haven't
even boned up on the old kind.
Hester told you, for example,
that all babies look like their daddies
for the first year so that their fathers
won't kill them. Uh-oh:
Some of us still, looking back,
look like our old man. Is this
why you've turned mean to me
as a rusty old bent nail?
It's hard, granted, for an introvert
to be a parent, and these are bad days,
I can see that, to be a hypochondriac.
I'm just trying to think the truth
in my own mind: the way red
fabric looks great on a woman's
skin . . . those two fluids, binary
explosives, constitute another foiled
plot: one's basic hurt. "It's Murphy's
Law, *whatevs* . . ." says a fellow passenger
going, like me, absolutely nowhere
because one obviously must go backward
to keep moving forward, which is key
to all real transit. No wonder some days
I feel like such a Freud, I mean fraud.
Even my oeuvre is all over,
my plosives expanded, my horizons
exploded. No, I did not try to hit
on her. That's all over, as well,
which is just as well. At my age they're
all pretty in pink; but lyrical? Hell.
Capable of devotion? All that perfume,

and lotion can't lather this old leather
anymore. As if they'd show me more
than just the door! Sudoku, loss
of libido, and far worse, I now wish
all the worst people all the best.
Is that not a palimpsest?
The guy next to me is coughing
on me . . . won't somebody show him
to his coffin, play him some King/Goffin
and send him packing so I don't have to hear
all this old-man hacking? It's like heckling
myself, like going incognito
when I don't even need to. So,
what's all this warfare for? Where's
my cane, Citizen? Don't send me limping
off again to war, I'm too old, and now
the train is finally moving again. It can't go
very far, but I've paid for my ticket,
and I start off on the right foot always.

Self Portrait in a Velvet Dress

Wrong sex, you sing.
Eh? Don't they know
what they're doing
at an autopsy?
I'll probably have to hold
my tongue, literally.

And anyway, why
shouldn't the neighbors'
dogs bark, their skinks
play basketball till all hours?
Thank God it's Friday.

Thank God for crisp
white wine, and pee.
If flotillas of good lucks
came trolling my way,
I'd simply say: I'm sick.

Even before I was ill,
I was disgusted.
Please please yourself,
to paraphrase wrongly
James Brown, the sill.

Sometimes when you think
you're being reasonable
you are ranting, you minx.
I'm composing a bloody raw
list of things I dare not mention.

That's where the whole show
ends, or so they say.
Gone are the noses of yesterday!

DIXIE FRIED

i.m. Alex Chilton, James Luther Dickinson,
Andy Hummel, and my dad

The diggery dawgs came, running spluttering mud,
paws a-flapping, and these bawds
run fast, for all which they are not what we would
call Pronto Pups not AKA corn dogs, pigs
on a stick, meat on a bone, finger-dinner, tube-
steak, Dixie fried, jelly of the humdinger gut-stringers.

Fare is what you pay to get on the bus,
it's not fair, it's not the State Fair, it's a fur piece
with its glissando spun memories, floss-
flared and stupid, co-sponsored by the FOOP
(Fraternal Order of Police) –

Please God, no ketchup, catsup, get your hands
up for only mooseturds, mustards stanky and sweet,
yaller, supperating for supper, wounded and grounded,
no, not a smack of pickle relish or nuthin: I commend
and command only this single condiment, followed,
if by anything, by a asspocket of whiskey and a Starlite mint.

. . . . but this is the Past, all dirt-eating, okra, and Slim Jims:
the fullest most exalted old Past. Forgive
my description of it, but don't think it was pity that I felt.
It was less than pity: more an immense sympathy
overflowing into these dog days of August,
a feeling that them grinning slavering rednecks, our hounds
have an aura of life and death, of dreams and digestion
and waking, of grazing and noshing and drinking. I raise

my Moon Pie and half-filled pitcher of RC Cola to your tin ears,
you bar band slackers, and swing through a ringing
sea of grass, in the shadows of poplars with bees swinking

in air, almost as abstract as a mud pie recipe. For you,
a shudder in the pretense of innocence, a shake
at the infinite appetites for marrow, meat, gristle, skin, I.E.
save the gizzards and reserve the liquid, 'cos
I'm a ding-dong daddy from Tennessee, I'm a mudboy
salivating for Pronto Pups, not AKA corn dogs I tell you what.

Carp Ascending a Waterfall

Grudging and begrudging me snow
       here where the broken water runs
(Grand Theft Auto . . . Shark Attack Pictures)
       and not in exile I reflect
that nobody in Ovid turns into
       their mother or father
gets diabetes / asthma / and/or thyroid
       problems, he had no
blog: I leave you mine, a hoarse man
       of the Apocalypse.

Or as Stein said, as Stein once said,
       what is the use of being
a boy if you are going to grow up
       to be a man . . . all I can say is
from Agincourt to Foodcourt, peel it and see!
       (Raisin in the Sun . . .
Stay Home Moms . . . Heidi Klum . . .
       The Ten Most Memorable
Pieces of Space Junk) – you can't copy-
       right titles: something
is fair use or public domain if you don't
       have to prove it isn't.

She was nice looking, so I looked
       at the nicelookingness
as the wind entered the train and walked
       around like a person
or the red-haired fox we see everywhere.
       Such are our non-traditional
allies, but Laconia where they all live
       is the opposite of Franconia.
I am laconic and frank myself (Dumpster
       Diving . . . Burger Recipes),

I let the chips fall where they may (Lasagna
        Recipes . . . Hepatitis C).
Why does everything cry, or want to?
        (Real Housewives . . .
Dungeons and Dragons) In answer

To which I propose that your top searches
        will not be recorded.
Your house is killing you, your child
        wants to keep you both together
the body wants to go, and I wish I would, then
        (Simple Living) . . . house fall down.
You don't want me to see what I don't see: OMG!
        (Neighbors Wonder How Captivity
Went Unnoticed for 24 Years). Scalded and scolded
        in the kitchen, the dreamtime archive
of ancient Greece tells us we're supposed to be
        solid gold for our kids, not hollow
chocolate Easter bunnies from the Jewel ("I'm self-
        ish, but in a good way!"). ("I go
to your house and I don't even get a fucking
        glass of water.") The cracks
in our ceiling are the avuncular handwriting
        of earlier tenants' last hours
and they spell out the question of whether
        God sees us, and how.

Maddy flies away on her red Radio Flyer scooter made
        in China, and nobody listens
to me or to the radio anymore, or wants to play
        hide-and-seek, just as lakes
are not the sea, rivers are not silver linings,
        and when the waterpipe burst
on the first thawy day it was like a lonely
        child playing or somebody

going the wrong direction on the train or
            shaking the hand of an Orthodox
woman who says softly, "Poetry and spirituality,
            how I hate that!" Or: "I never suspect
venomous creatures live here" (that's original
            sin for you), "or any insect or
animal that has yet to speak its first word." For

I can't think in this badly defrosted car, and the other
            riders must certainly know something
I don't; even my own father doesn't remember
            his own dead sister, and I all know
is that her name was Anita, simple as a pail
            and shovel and sand and shells,
isn't it? (Employers May Still Hire You Without
            a Degree) My family tree,
dismantled, nothing left to climb: who made
            that big mistake? How small
are grass seeds, my daughter rightly asks, not
            getting any traction, and I think
only one of us will survive to eulogize the other.
            All as it should be. I don't
recall your real name, or what I was going
            to do today, but I do remember
            UL9-0910.
The Creator is not responsible for lost or stolen
            items. *Item:* the fallen
angels aren't talking . . .

*

Radiant thaw –
            missing exemplary objects
            snakeholing crap

The dead bird
        in a different place
                on the pavement today

Who sang, "Hey. . .
        You. . .
                Get Off Of My Cloud."

The wrecks,
        runners and junks
                on their way to work

Saying: "I lost weight
        with an all-natural
                secret weapon."

Heavy smoke
        could be seen for blocks,
                the machinery, the mechanism

Brooding block women
        have the trick:
                "How can you know

The word if you never heard it?"

*

Sleeping furiously, desperate measures, fractured
        tasks, essays in criticism –
How dare you lecture me about indeterminacy
        or even be right about anything?
Shut off the water at the cutoff and bleed
        the pipes: "You haven't had
to do SO much for my family," she said.

Nobody says my name. Don't say my name.
    This is nothing resembling
a bequest, I am not an organ donor nor
    even pee when I need to
and I'm not fucking coming back (Mystery
    of Absinthe's Mind-Altering
Effects May Have Been Solved at Last),
    that's the one good thing
I know, I mean, even King David got into
    trouble for his Psalms, last
of the upper worlds, first of the lower.
    First my dad lost a sister
then my mom lost a brother then I lost
    a sister and had a sick
brother, then you came along –
    my spirit fled from the mount
into the desert, such is my androcentric nature,
    unfixed . . . Hello,

Exilio! Which is why I love sleep so much,
    even the nightmares,
and seldom actually get there, or adore
    food in my old age and
eat so badly: it's that easy to damage persons
    but don't let that fool you:
Whatever power I had was ironized long ago.
    Teach me, then, how to
grieve and sulk like you (Boy With Half
    a Brain Plays Tennis, Solves
Equations); I mean, what am I separating
    myself from, hanging on
every word like that? Oh. My life. Or at least
    my vegetable soul.

Down the road I go, ramble-tamble, to the new
    figuration. I did not expect

love to corrode the red Radio Flyer, or to be
        listened to, much. Somebody
here in Minneapolis thumbed black
        The Collected Books
of Jack Spicer, but the bridge Berryman went
        over still looks modern.
(I'm ashamed to look, so I didn't even look.
        And time runs out
for looking, as for everything else, you know.)
        "These Hebrews in their graves,
how can they rise?" With pinch points and body
        language: "take off your shoes by
the Burning Bush," and where are those among
        whom we can sit down and weep?
Rabbi Eleazer said: From the day on which
        the Temple was destroyed
the gates of prayer have been closed . . . But
        though the gates of prayer
are closed, the gates of weeping are not closed.

About suffering he was never wrong, Joe-the-Plumber.

Provide, provide –

The two saddest words in the language.

FANTASIA ON THE RAPTURE

You know that part of a movie where
it's almost over, but

not quite? And you're glad? Well, that
is where I am with life.

The horror of just being a line, or being
contracted into a line, a line

that shatters into a thousand aberrations –
I could not even retreat dead

into emotion, so . . . Measure my life
in occupations and recycling instead.

I had learned to dissemble, *mon frère*!
And if I had any real

gumption, I'd machine-gun that great
big collected poems of so-and-so.

"We have come," Yeats was told by
the unknown writer,

"to give you metaphors for poetry."
Like him, my wife tells me,

I have been engaged in bouts
of snoring, of "sleaps,"

of dreams with sounds, hallucinations,
scents, flashes of light,

and movements of external objects, namely
mosquitos and cats.

On whose esoteric authority are we
to accept all this rapture?

Isn't it all just a hearty bit of *temps
perdu*? I eat. Pray. Leave.

I asked for some TLC, but all I got was
The Learning Channel.

Well, life is nothing if not edu-
cational. Cultural

crapital . . . Absolutitis . . . I don't believe
that an individual is

the result of a crowd of a million
divided by a million,

and I don't believe in pinning you
down like a butterfly, or know how

many stars should be in
the evening sky before we start to pray.

But I do know that *affliction most doe
give us eyes to see.*

Lines Written During Harvest Time

In my mind,
it's almost pumpkin pie time.

The lattes are on the froth,
and Mr. Blue Sky has banged

his fists purple on a table
amply set for two.

Tropic of corn sugar,
black spring of Tropicana,

let's face it: I don't need God
because every time I move

something, you're the one
who notices it. I'm filled

with thanksgiving, and though sad
have quit saying Kaddish for Dad.

DED (Dutch Elm Disease)

The town came round and said
our tree must come down –
Like a bell without a clapper,
this yard without its elm.

LOOKING OVER MY SHOULDER

I went to Heaven once, sadly
leaving my push-mower and orange snow
shovel behind, like uneaten food
pushed aside on a stark china plate.

The man upstairs was not happy.
He liked a sharp blade and a clear
driveway. His strictures were

stringent enough to shrive a cactus.
Yet it was I who blindly insisted
on formalities, and stood

on what I thought was ceremony.
I could scarcely taste the beer he poured,
or eat my ham sandwich.

When our visit was over,
he shook my hand and sent me
somersaulting back to my village, where

I was filled, thank God, with genuine salt.

ACKNOWLEDGMENTS

"Waterfall Ascending a Carp" and "Flip-Flops and Mary Janes" were published in *Fulcrum 7*; "High Holidays," "The Crew Change," and "Wishbone" were published in *The Common*; "Wishbone" appeared on the Poetry Daily website as a poem of the day and is included in the anthology, *City of the Big Shoulders: An Anthology of Chicago Poetry*, ed. Ryan Van Cleave (University of Iowa Press, 2012); "The Crew Change" and "Rice in the Spoon" appeared in the *Paris Review* blog; "On Being Philosophical" appeared in *Jacket;* "DED (Dutch Elm Disease)" appeared on the *Verse* website; "Stonecrop" appeared online in *The Rumpus;* "Civilization and its Discontents" appeared online in *Cellpoems*; "Symbiosis" appeared in *Tuesday: An Art Project*; "To the Sister I Never Had" appeared in *Literary Imagination*; "Self Portrait in a Velvet Dress" appeared in *The Equalizer*; "High Holidays" and "DED (Dutch Elm Disease)" was also published in *Brute Neighbors: Urban Nature Poetry, Prose & Photography*, edited by Chris Green (DePaul University Humanities Center Poetry Institute, 2011); "Looking over My Shoulder" first appeared in the anthology, *Joining Music with Reason: 34 Poets, British and American,* chosen by Christopher Ricks (Waywiser Press, 2010); Some of the poems in the first section were published in a chapbook, *The Traumatophile* (Scantily Clad Press, 2009); "On Thanksgiving" was published as a broadside by the Woodland Pattern Poetry Center; "Dixie Fried" was a commission for Roddy Lumsden's "Lardermania" event, held in London on May 14, 2010, and the poem was published in *Magna*; "Poetry" was published in *this corner* (Green Issue), edited by John Kinsella and Rod Mengham. A section of "Briefs" won the *Writer's Digest* Poetic Form Challenge for a "Lune."

DON SHARE is Senior Editor of *Poetry* magazine in Chicago. His collections of poetry include *Squandermania* (Salt Publishing, 2007) and *Union* (Zoo Press, 2002). His other books include a critical edition of Basil Bunting's poems (forthcoming from Faber & Faber), *Bunting's Persia* (Flood Editions, 2012), *Seneca in English* (Penguin Classics, 1998), and Miguel Hernández's *I Have Lots of Heart* (Bloodaxe Books, 1997), which was awarded the *Times Literary Supplement* Translation Prize, the Premio Valle Inclán, and the PEN/New England "Discovery" Award. With Christian Wiman, he co-edited *The Open Door: 100 Years, 100 Poems from Poetry Magazine* (University of Chicago Press, 2012).

A NOTE ON THE TYPE

WISHBONE *has been set in Mercury Text, a family of types originally developed by Tobias Frere-Jones for the* New Times *newspaper chain. Faced with the variability of printing multiple editions in different regions, the* New Times *needed types that would print well under less-than-ideal conditions and that could effectively handle a demanding range of types of information, from headlines to dense financial data. Careful legibility research, followed by extensive press testing, led to the creation of a family of "graded" types – types that increased in degree of darkness, but not in weight or set width – that would perform reliably throughout the paper's operations.* ⫶⫶ *In other enviroments, Mercury's crisp drawing, characterized by taut curves and neat wedge serifs, makes for an elegant page, one that encourages effortless reading while retaining a distinct typographic identity.*

DESIGN, COMPOSITION, & LETTERING BY CARL W. SCARBROUGH